It's Time to Celebrate

EASTER

Written by
Rebecca Phillips-Bartlett

KidHaven
PUBLISHING

Published in 2026 by
KidHaven Publishing, an Imprint of
Greenhaven Publishing, LLC
2544 Clinton St., Buffalo, NY 14224

Written by: Rebecca Phillips-Bartlett
Edited by: Noah Leatherland
Designed by: Ker Ker Lee

All facts, statistics, web addresses, and URLs in this book were verified as valid and accurate at time of writing. No responsibility for any changes to external websites or references can be accepted by either the author or publisher.

Cataloging-in-Publication Data
Names: Phillips-Bartlett, Rebecca.
Title: Easter / Rebecca Phillips-Bartlett.
Description: Buffalo, NY : Kidhaven Publishing, 2026. | Series: Its time to celebrate | Includes index and glossary
Identifiers: ISBN 9781534550063 (pbk) | ISBN 9781534550070 (library bound) | ISBN 9781534550087 (ebook)
Subjects: LCSH: Easter--Juvenile Literature | Easter Bunny—Juvenile Literature | Holidays—Juvenile Literature
Classification: LCC GT4930 P45 2026 | DDC 394.2667 --dc25

Manufactured in the United States of America

CPSIA compliance information: Batch #CSKH26
For further information contact Greenhaven Publishing LLC at 1-844-317-7404.

Please visit our website, www.greenhavenpublishing.com.
For a free color catalog of all our high-quality books, call toll free 1-844-317-7404 or fax 1-844-317-7405.

Find us on

Photo Credits – Images are courtesy of Shutterstock.com. With thanks to Getty Images, Thinkstock Photo, and iStockphoto.

Recurring images – KanKhem, miumi, Smilingirida. Cover – AnastasiiaM Studio, BNP Design Studio. 2–3 – ShineTerra. 4–5 – Gabriela Bertolini, Thoom. 6–7 – rudall30. 8–9 – Evgeny Atamanenko, Mircea Moira, Sara Carpenter. 10–11 – AnjelikaGr, Nomad_Soul. 12–13 – ShineTerra, Teguh Mujiono. 14–15 – Olya Detry. 16–17 – BlueOrange Studio, Fotiy_Svetlana. 18–19 – Serenko Natalia, Studio QUB. 20–21 – Diane Diederich, Ken Griffiths, Milleflore Images, Sandra Foyt. 22–23 – PhotoJuli86, wavebreakmedia.

Contents

Words that look like <u>this</u> can be found in the glossary on page 24.

It's Almost Easter!

Hi! My name is Demi. It is nearly Easter. Easter is a Christian festival when we remember the end of Jesus Christ's life on Earth. In Christianity, Jesus is known as the son of God.

Easter is a time of reflection and remembrance for Christians.

The 40 days before Easter are known as Lent. The day before Lent is called Shrove Tuesday. It is also known as Mardi Gras. Lent starts on Ash Wednesday, which is usually in February.

During Lent, Christians remember Jesus's last days on Earth.

The Easter Story

When Jesus was alive on Earth, he taught God's messages. However, leaders at the time did not agree with these messages. They punished Jesus by putting him on a cross. This is called crucifixion.

The day Jesus was crucified is called Good Friday.

When Jesus died, his followers buried him in a cave. The next Sunday, they visited the cave. The stone door had moved and Jesus's body was gone. An angel told them that Jesus had risen.

Coming back to life is called resurrection.

Celebrating Easter

Holy Week starts with a happy day called Palm Sunday.

Easter is one of the most important Christian festivals. The week before Easter is called Holy Week. During Holy Week, Christians remember Jesus's last week on Earth. Some days are happy. Some remember sad events.

Jesus's resurrection is celebrated on Easter Sunday. Easter is a very happy day celebrating new life. On Easter Sunday, many Christians go to church. Many people celebrate with Easter eggs.

Cooking Corner

Let's Make Chocolate Nests

You will need:

- 1/2 pound bag (225 g) of chocolate
- 2 2/3 cups (75 g) of cornflakes
- 2 tablespoons (30 mL) of light corn syrup
- 1 3/4 cups (50 g) of butter
- Mini chocolate eggs
- Cupcake wrappers

How to make chocolate nests:

1. Heat some water in a saucepan until it is simmering.
2. Put the chocolate, corn syrup, and butter in a large bowl. Put the bowl on top of the pan of water. Stir until the mixture has melted.
3. Take the bowl off the heat. Gently mix the cereal into the melted mixture.
4. Spoon the chocolatey cereal into 12 cupcake wrappers. Decorate with chocolate eggs.
5. Leave in the fridge for one hour to set.

A Visit from the Easter Bunny

Have you ever eaten a chocolate Easter egg? It could have been delivered by the Easter Bunny. The Easter Bunny brings treats to children on Easter Sunday. Sometimes, the treats come in baskets that are hidden!

Easter eggs are a symbol of Jesus's resurrection on Easter Sunday. Bunnies and eggs are both symbols of new life and the season of spring, which is when Easter is celebrated.

Craft Corner

Let's Make Easter Bunny Bunting

You will need:

- Colored paper
- Scissors
- String
- Glue
- Cotton balls

How to make bunny bunting:

1. Draw the <u>outline</u> of an Easter bunny on a piece of paper. Cut it out.
2. Use this bunny as a <u>template</u> to draw more bunnies. Cut them out.

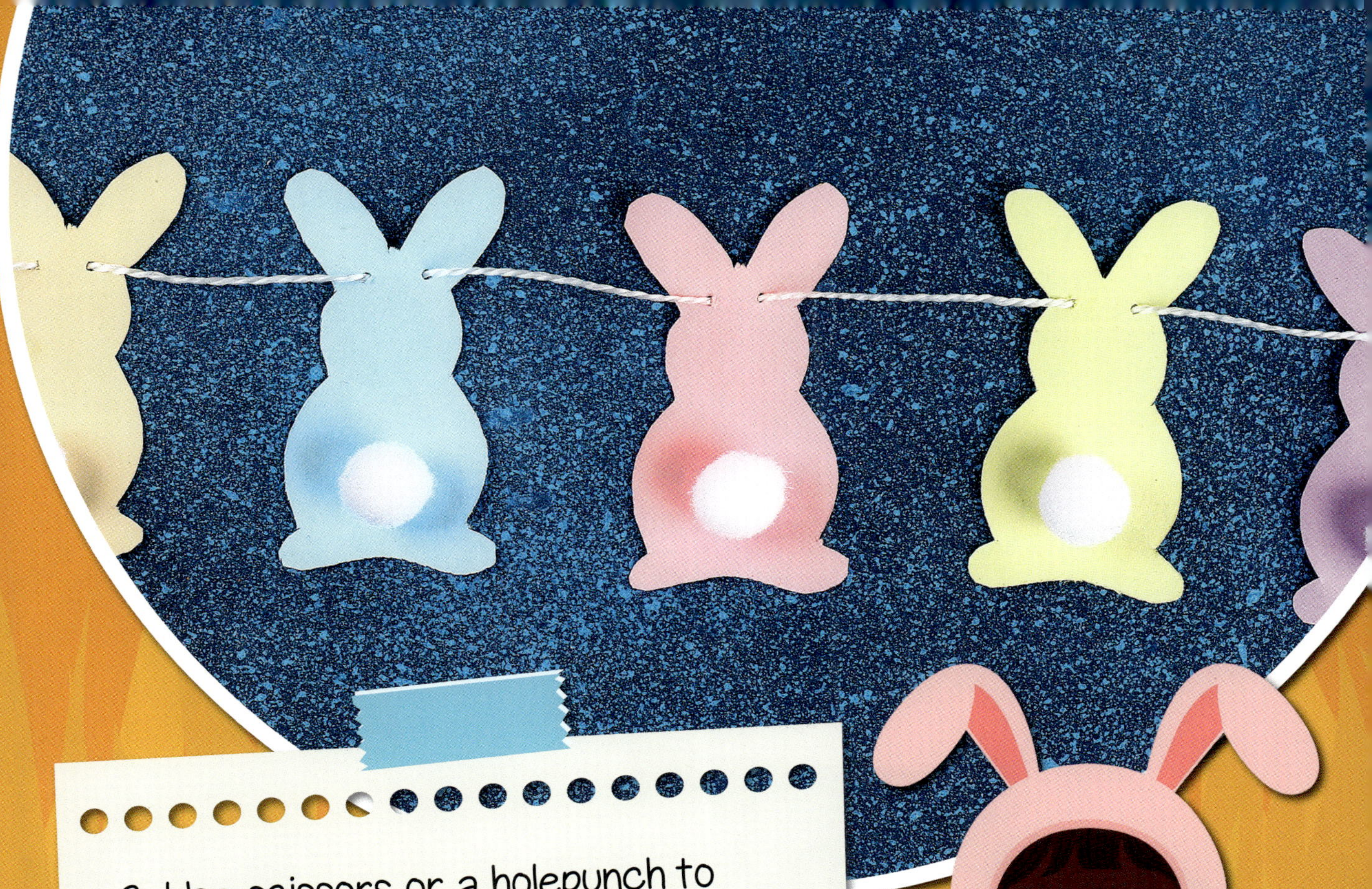

3. Use scissors or a holepunch to make two holes in the top of each bunny.
4. Thread string through each hole. Spread the shapes along the string.
5. Glue a cotton ball tail onto each bunny.

On Easter Sunday

For my family, Easter Sunday starts with a trip to church. During Lent, the church is usually decorated in purple. However, by Easter Sunday the church is full of flowers and gold decorations.

At church, we listen to Bible stories and sing happy Easter songs.

In the afternoon, I meet up with my friends. We have an Easter egg hunt to find eggs in the garden.

Activity Corner

Let's Plan an Easter Egg Hunt

You will need:

- Easter eggs
- Easter baskets or buckets
- Friends to join in

You could use:

- Paper
- A pen or pencil

How to plan an Easter egg hunt:

1. Count the Easter eggs so you know how many you have.
2. Hide the Easter eggs around the garden or house.
3. You could write some clues about the eggs' hiding places.
4. Invite your friends over to find the Easter eggs!

Easter Around the World

Many countries all over the world have their own Easter traditions.

Chocolate bunnies are a popular Easter treat in many countries. In Australia, they eat chocolate bilbies instead. Bilbies are endangered in parts of Australia.

On Good Friday, many people in Bermuda fly homemade kites as a symbol of Jesus rising to heaven.

On Easter Monday, the President of the United States holds an egg roll. People roll eggs along the grass using a spoon.

It's Time to Celebrate Easter

There are lots of ways to celebrate Easter. Now you know the Easter story and how some people choose to celebrate, so there is only one thing left to do. It is time to celebrate Easter!

Do you have any Easter or Lent traditions? Perhaps you visit church with your family or have exciting Easter egg hunts with your friends. It is never too late to start your own family traditions!

Glossary

endangered	when a type of animal is in danger of dying out
heaven	the place where gods live in many religions
outline	a line showing the shape of something
reflection	serious thought
remembrance	the act of remembering something
season	different parts of the year based on changes in the weather and amount of sunlight
simmering	cooking on a low heat to make small bubbles
template	a piece of material used as an outline to create more of the same thing
traditions	beliefs and actions that are passed down between people over time

Index